THE LITANY OF THE GREAT RIVER

MEINRAD CRAIGHEAD

Paulist Press
New York,
Mahwah, N.J.

Other books by Meinrad Craighead

The Mother's Birds
The Sign of the Tree
The Mother's Songs
Images of God the Mother
Liturgical Art

Cover and interior design by Meinrad Craighead

Library of Congress Cataloging-in-Publication Data

Craighead, Meinrad.
    The litany of the great river/by Meinrad Craighead.
        p.   cm.
    ISBN 0-8091-0448-2
        1. Meditations.   I. Title.
    BX2182.2.C72   1991
    242—dc20   90-21715
                                                              CIP

Published by Paulist Press
997 Macarthur Boulevard
Mahwah, N.J. 07430

Printed and bound in the United States of America

For EM
RM and RL
Coyote and Badger
13th April 1989

CONTENTS

Remembering the Litany _____ 8

THE LITANY

Heart of the Fire _____ 14

Holy Mountain _____ 16

Rain from Heaven _____ 18

Eternal Presence _____ 20

Porta Coeli _____ 22

Eye of Heaven _____ 24

Sacred Hearts _____ 27

Cave of the Heart _____ 28

Waters of Salvation _____ 30

Guardian of the Land _____ 32

Eternal Water _____ 35

Soul of the World _____ 36

Call of the Wild _____ 38

Guardian of the Place _____ 40

Hidden Garden _____ 42

Seat of Wisdom ———————————— 44

Wellspring ———————————————— 46

Alma Mater ———————————————— 48

Holy Trinity ———————————————— 51

Rosa Mystica ——————————————— 52

You Who Give the Dream ——————— 54

Beauty of the Deep ————————————— 56

Place of Emergence ———————————— 58

Origin of the Journey ————————— 60

Tree of Paradise ———————————— 62

Eye of the Earth ————————————— 64

Sound in the Stones ———————————— 66

Guardian of the Dance —————————— 68

Desire of the Eternal Hills —————— 70

O Fountain Mouth ————————————— 72

Catalogue of the Paintings ——— 75–76

R E M E M B E R I N G
T H E   L I T A N Y

Some years ago my aunt in Little Rock cleaned her attic and the next generation became the guardians of the family memorabilia. My sisters and cousins and I were the new custodians of the unremarkable things worthy of keeping and remembering. Living in England at the time, and vowed to poverty, I was sent a slight but fitting and deeply meaningful piece of the family estate, my grandmother's old prayerbook. Grandpa had used it until he died in 1952.

Between The Most Necessary Prayers (there are fifteen of these) and Various Prayers (twenty-six) are the Litanies. There are four litanies in my grandmother's prayerbook: of the Holy Name of Jesus, of the Sacred Heart of Jesus, of the Blessed Virgin Mary, of Saint Joseph. Probably because it is lengthy, the Litany of All Saints is not included.

I had not prayed these litanies since childhood and then never privately. Few Catholics who were children in the 1940s can forget those holy days when we processed (a single file of girls on one side of the aisle, boys on the other, the youngest children leading) up, around and down the aisles of our parish church, repeating this path for the duration of the litany.

The litanies were the extra special public prayers. The pews were filled; the entire parish always seemed to be in church for the choral recitation. Carefully groomed and dressed in spotless school uniforms we children moved forward, sometimes carrying candles, chanting the somber Latin litanies phrase by phrase, step by step. We called out the poetic refrains: *Sancta Maria* and *Rosa Mystica*, *Stella Matutina* and *Porta Coeli* and were answered by the parishioners who completed each petition: *ora pro nobis, te rogamus audi nos* or *exaudi nos*. Step, pause, recite, response, we moved in solemn measured procession, taking the parishioners, our families, on a journey. We led them on a pilgrimage into another place and we went there together, chanting the familiar Latin litanies.

Feasts of Jesus, feasts of Our Blessed Mother, feasts of the saints, we all knew the litanies for these feasts by heart, as did the entire congregation who also had chanted them since childhood.

When the litanies were chanted at night, after Benediction, a Forty Hours Devotion or a Novena to Our Lady or another saint, the night seemed to further empower the ritual. Entering from the dark streets we found the church already filled with candles burning, a divine waste that seemed to confirm the purity of the sacred action we anticipated. And leaving, after the service ended, was a kind of exile, a return to darkness and homework.

No ceremony in the Catholic Church affected me so profoundly as the communal recitation of these litanies through the round of the liturgical year. I shall never forget the impact this invocation from the Litany of the Sacred Heart had on me: *Desire of the Eternal Hills, have mercy on us.*

Many years later a professor in an art history class spoke of "the principle of indefinite extension" and I remembered the procession of the litanies. The long series of invocations and supplications with their alternate responses moving us forward and around was like the repetition of the multiple columns and windows in a church or the procession of thousands of repeated patterned tiles in a mosque, individual units multiplied, moving in orderly progression toward infinity.

Repetition of a sacred formula mesmerized us. The very monotony shifted us into a different mood. The rhythmical flow and the precise syllables of the sacred language got inside our bodies; the step-pause-recite-pause-response movements were as regular and drumlike as our heartbeats. All the spirits and holy ancestors we were invoking seemed to walk along with us, our remembering them made them present. We pulled them back into time and they invited us into eternity. We were "indefinitely extended" by those litanies.

They are long since gone from common use in the Church, but the memory of them infuses the rhythm of my daily prayer. Outside at my fire altar each morning, I am still moving around a sacred space, continuing an unbroken journey, speaking a litany, letting the word images run into the land and rest in the air and mingle with the sound of the Rio Grande flowing just to the west.

When I attend the ceremonial dances of the Pueblo people here in the valley of the Rio Grande, the hypnotic pattern of the measured steps and repeated evocative chant of the litanies comes to mind. Winter and summer, day and night, up and down the valley, their sacred sounds and movements and mimetic gestures call down the heavens and bring up the earth throughout the seasons. Simultaneously secret and communal, each drummer and each chanter, each dancer is a binding link between these two realms, receiving the descending and ascending blessings for the good of all life. The spacious openness of the New Mexican landscape defines the naked division of heaven and earth. On top of earth, at the bottom of heaven, the divine is called forth by the numbing repetition of sound and step unchanged through generations. The drumming reaches far out to embrace this pale, empty land with its distant mountains and pull them to the hallowed center of prayer.

Season after season these Pueblo people sing and dance in thanksgiving with antelope and deer, turtle, buffalo, butterfly and eagle. They have learned what the animals have taught them. They hide with Fox. They see with Owl and sleep with Mole. They dance with Snake, play with Otter and grin with Coyote. They heal with Badger root medicine and sing down the rains with Frog. With Spider they spin and weave. With Turtle spirit they shape their pots. In dreaming Bear heart they hear the deepest drum song. Wild Turkey shows them the proud wildness of creation. They watch with Crow and Raven and listen with Mountain Lion. Beaver teaches them to build and Buffalo to give their all. With Horse they run. With Eagle they soar. Wolf teaches them to teach.

In story and song, dance and chant, each animal is summoned, a re-vered messenger from the Great Spirit, a carrier of the sacred, a word from God about God. But it is not a word, it is a beak or a claw, a shell or a quill, feather or fur, a wing or a tail or a hoof which carries the divine message to us: Love them, they too are my soul.

Perhaps the ear of my heart is attuned to the teachings of these Native American people through my father's remote Chickasaw heritage. Surely within my morning litany, inspired by my Catholicism, there flows a rhythm of imagery and sound which rises from other ancestral memories. *O Thou Guardian of the Land, O Thou Sound in the Stones, O Thou Heart of the Fire, O Thou Fountain Mouth* I have said, binding the earth, air, fire and water into my prayer with other images, other memo-ries, other experiences.

Quite often at the fire in the morning I recall scraps of songs which, as a child, I sang with my mother and grandmother. "Down in the Valley," *O Thou Valley.* "I'm bringing you a big bouquet of roses," *O Thou Rose.* And most often "Shall we gather at the River," which we always danced as we sang. "Shall we gather at the River, the beautiful, the beautiful River." *O Thou River.*

The movement in my soul which I first named was water. The stirrings felt like water and from an early age the waters poured out as imagery. I began drawing pictures. My mother once told me that I was a noisy infant, not a cryer, but a crooner, humming and babbling. She liked to sing to me because I wanted to sing with her. But one day I fell silent and passed into a different place where I was happiest being left alone to draw. When she told me this she became sad, perhaps reliving the memory of her young daughter withdrawing from her. She said, almost accusingly (and I was over forty years old at the time), "When you began to draw you stopped singing."

I have often wondered if this disposition to watery imagery springs from a lingering memory of my prenatal growth and birth experience. Or should I believe the astrologers who call me Aquarian? While I took my mother's blood and breath and then her milk, were the February stars pouring waters into my nascent imagination?

Before I could read, when words were only sounds, not yet ciphers in a book, when words arrived as melodies to my ears before my eyes could decipher them, I heard a word which forever made of word, water and God one round whole. Lying with my dog beneath blue hydrangeas in my grandmother's garden, shaded against a hot Arkansas afternoon, what I heard within my little girl body was the sound of rushing water. And in the roar, ebbing and flowing as I listened, a word: Come. And I knew that the watery word was God.

Born into a Catholic family, it was in the psalms that I first experienced poetry. Here I found words which enabled me to name the movements of my soul, follow them, understand and believe them. In the psalm verses the singers spoke of things which were already stirring me. Trees and rivers, birds and animals, mountains and temples were huge, expansive, inside my body. The drumming of the many single syllable words, blood and bone, gate, fire, dark, hammered like my own heartbeats.

The words of the psalms were not just sounds; the words were images, images of the world, images of God. The brief verses flashed in and out of the liturgy of the Catholic mass like bright melodic intrusions into the long rhetorical portions of the service. They told me that rivers clapped their hands and trees shouted for joy, hills leapt like yearling lambs and heaven sang. Days told stories and messages blew through the night wind. God had wings and I could hide within them. There was an apple in God's eye and I was inside the apple. I was the watered hills and the tree planted beside flowing water which would yield fruit in due season. I never doubted this. I drew water from a deep well and knew that it was my birthright.

The psalmists sang songs of remembering. Songs of thanksgiving are songs of remembering. We give memories to our souls and our souls weave them, thread by thread, into the amazing garment of our unique identity. We say to our souls: I am myself because these are my memories, this is my cloak of many colors and I can tell you a story about every thread. Because I am an artist I unwind the threads and investigate the patterns; I wonder about the colors and feel the textures. Like all artists I tell my story because I know that personal memories have the power to speak to others. Everyone recognizes songs of remembering.

There is a story from northern European mythology about the god Odin who lived alone in the highest branches of the great World Tree. The Tree was rooted in the center of the earth and reached beyond seeing into the heavens. Odin relied on his two ravens to fly off at dawn and return at dusk to pass the night telling him stories about life down on earth. He called his ravens Thought and Memory. One morning after the ravens had flown off to view the world, Odin had a terrible thought. He asked himself, "Should one of my ravens perish, which raven could I live without?" He brooded and finally spoke to the leaves, "I fear for my Thought, lest he come not back, but I fear yet more for my Memory."

My mother was not quite right. I did not stop singing. The humming stayed inside, the watery sounds collected around the place in my soul where imagery was to gather and focus in memories, in paintings. The sounds and the imagery rose from the same source. It was water which first told me that I was an artist and I believed the water.

O HEART OF THE FIRE
sear us, we beseech Thee

When the sun rises over the Sandia Mountains, a fire burns facing it. My morning prayer begins with this fire burning in a gourd-shaped terra-cotta vessel. What falls from the nine great cottonwood trees on my land feeds it day by day. The small fire burns in the gourd's belly; flames and smoke rise from the neck. The oven sits on a square altar built over the bones and black feathers of a crow who died here soon after I arrived. Crow needed to be buried.

Gradually the grave became the place where I always stood and prayed each morning, my body a prayer stick, in the center of this specific place. In 1986, my 50th birthday approached and with it a growing understanding that I needed to mark this lifeline and to step over it into a final phase of thanksgiving for my life. I decided to build the altar over Crow's grave.

On twelve large terracotta tiles, embedded in the adobe stucco of the four sides of the altar, I painted designs which beg gifts from the cross of the four directions.

When I approach my altar in the dark before dawn, before I lay the cottonwood kindling and light the fire, I take ashes from yesterday's fire and rub them on my forehead (if every day is Resurrection, every day is Ash Wednesday). By the time I have made my sacred prayer circle, the fire has burned to embers. I end my prayer with water. I baptize myself. I say, ''Meinrad, you are sealed. You belong to God. You drink her milk and her tears and you shed her blood. She looks at you. Because she looks at you, you paint.'' I throw the remaining water into the dying fire to hear the sound of the union and watch steam fill the belly of the vessel. Before long, in this high desert climate, the ash is gray dry, the bed for tomorrow's fire.

O HOLY MOUNTAIN
bear us, we beseech Thee

The east face of the altar receives first light. I watch the dark eastern sky over the Sandia Mountains fade into grays and then spread searing pinks and yellows before the rising sun. Sun rises from the Womb Below, open fire eye burning in the Womb Above, traveling west in its proud overarching journey, warming the egg of the world and hatching the miracles of creation before it falls down into the body of night, exhausted. My morning prayer begins here at the east, a meditation on the blessings which rise up and fall down each day, in the Beginning.

O RAIN FROM HEAVEN
temper us, we beseech Thee

Turning south is going into the day, chasing zenith power. Images of Sun and Full Moon, side by side, are painted on this side of the altar. The impossible Winged Serpent sweeps the energies of our sky lights into unity and charges earth in its eternal cycle, swallowing the end of its journey so that it may begin, again and again. All day the unblinking sun runs down the moon and gazehound chases hare. They all run with the energies of the day. The day is the doing of it (What did you do today?) for most of us. The meditation for the south is a question: How will I receive today? What will I make this day? Hare runs into my studio and waits for me.

O ETERNAL PRESENCE

measure us, we beseech Thee

Standing before the west face of the altar is to think about the End, which is union. The pictures here repeat those on the east face of the altar, but in reverse. Here the water does not rain vertically, the water flows horizontally. It is the water lying in earth, a river running to its source. It is one river merging with all rivers to become one body of water lying just over the horizon (which is everywhere at eye level). Turtle crawls down underground, into Demeter's domain, to wait through the dark half of our year. With her winged horns the full moon embraces her sisters. They are herself, her other eyes. The old sickle moon looks back to her virgin aspect and thinks, My, how time flies. She is grandmother now, flying into oblivion. Snake carries West to the End where we all go to sleep, to die, to drop off the edge with sun into Beginning.

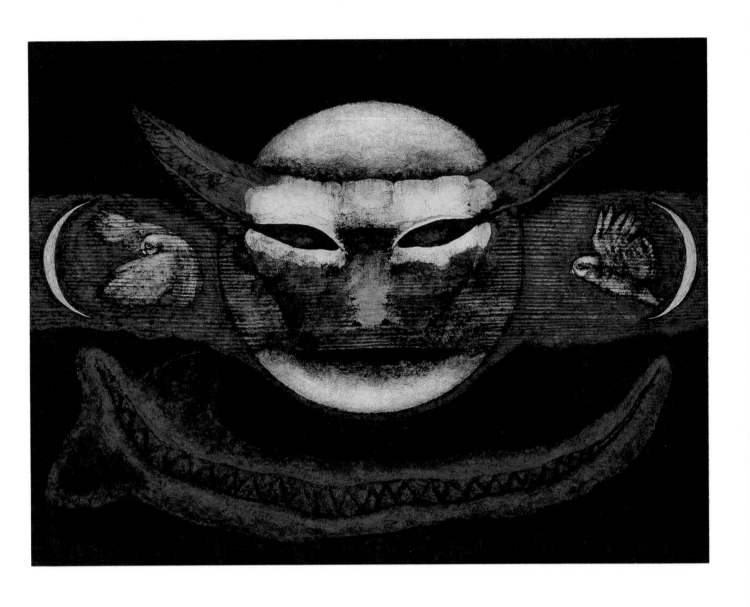

O PORTA COELI
open us, we beseech Thee

Finally I am standing at the north face of the altar. Nadir completes the cycle. Nadir is under my feet. O Thou Void, black hole surrounded by the brightest stars. O Thou Darkness, you deepest downreach, you furthest outreach, you abysmal inreach, you otherland which leads to the gateway of her body.

The guardian dogs which lead your children back home are howling. They near the arch, they are closing on the scent. Unbinding your hair you overshadow your creatures and welcome them into your lap.

O EYE
OF HEAVEN
attend us, we beseech Thee

When I leave my fire altar I go into my studio and begin another day of painting. My studio is named for Maat, the All Seeing Eye of the Mother. I paint within her eye and she watches me. What more may I say of this Mother than, She keeps an eye on me. As her eye gives birth to me, my eyes bring out my images. The feather of her flying eye, seeking truth, falls on my brush. I built this space, this place, to encircle the eye of her presence. This is our home. This is it, my cell, where I live alone with her.

She sows her magic beans, claiming my soil, possessing my womanhood. She feeds me from her abundant lap. She feeds me white maize and yellow maize, red maize and her precious blue maize. She stuffs the colors into my center and I mix my inks. Outside crows gather in the cottonwoods, throwing their eyes around, scanning this river valley. What they see they talk about. They tell us what they see. Flying between me and the southern sun, their ragged shadows pass over my work bench, altering colors, suggesting values, changing patterns.

The studio was named and blessed and a figure of Maat placed on the seventh altar at the Vernal Equinox. My friends joined me and we entered in procession, bearing the stone animals and other sacred objects for the seven altars. The animals had come home to live with me inside the Eye of the All Seeing Mother.

O SACRED HEARTS

stir us, we beseech You

Before going to my workbench I circle Maat and feed her animals. The litany begun outside continues inside as I go around the seven altars, giving her animals cornmeal and juniper berries. I place each small stone fetish to my lips. I suck in its breath.

O Thou, brother Wolf, animal spirit of the white East, we need your yellow eyes to see the first light. We need your sight to create. You carry us journeying East of the Sun.

You, father Coyote, spirit of the red South, you run laughing into the sun and it spins for us, you poke the clouds and it rains for us, you sing and we hear the prophecies. You make us laugh, Coyote.

O Thou Bear, great Bear Mother of the blue West, you bring us into your heart cave, you send us healing dreams, you carry us journeying West of the Moon.

O Thou, Mountain Lion, Grandmother of the yellow North, guardian of the high, faraway rim-rock cave where the mysteries unfold. We crawl into your shining presence terrified of your truth and grace, your balance and your roaring beauty, of your claws and piercing cat eyes. But as we approach, you will lift your red ochre veil.

You, Eagle, great Grandfather of the all-color Zenith over our heads. Call us to live in the shelter of your healing wings. Take up our eyes and fix them with your wide focus. Guardian spirit of the winds, weave us within the invisible threads of your flight.

Mole, Toad and Turtle of the black Nadir beneath our feet, what do you hear in the wet darkness, my sisters? Have you heard her heartbeat drumming at the source? Tell us the secrets you have uncovered in the bowels of the earth. Burrow into our dreams and uncover our healing roots.

Without animals to share the motions of our lives we are diminished, our lives are less than whole. This impoverishment is one of our saddest and loneliest bargains with civilization. Surely, the goodness and beauty of this land of New Mexico is maintained, indeed stayed up, by the indigenous people. Rooted in this landscape from the beginning, they continue to celebrate and share their living vision of the place of animals in religion. Their chanted stories and sacred dance ceremonials, which link all creatures endowed with eyes and breath and heartbeat, bespeak a time when the world was not divided into animal and human, divine and non-divine. A time when boundaries were so fluid we all flowed in and out of each other and shone with equal light. A time when we understood the animals when they spoke to us and taught us how to survive and how to worship. But time shifted and drew distinctions. Time began to mark categories and the motion of the whole broke to pieces in words. What we named was separateness.

Yet our common needs and determined deaths link us. Our common life source declares our union. We are promised to each other and to believe this covenant is to love our animal wits and blessed instincts and sensual bodies.

O CAVE
OF THE HEART
illumine us, we beseech Thee

Who are these animals to whom I speak each morning? While the building of Maat was underway I wondered which animals would choose to

live in her. My totem animals are ever with me, again and again manifest in my dreams, Turtle, Horse and Mountain Lion, who travel in my dreamscapes and teach me. Would they guard this space alone? I made a Winter Solstice pilgrimage to Zuni Pueblo to spend the day with the stone animal fetishes which these people carve. If I spent time with these spirit animals they would answer my question, Do you want to come live with me? For a long time that day I handled the stone animals. Gradually the animals came. Wolf came first and the others followed, Bear, Coyote, Eagle, Mole and Toad. I brought them home and buried them near the foundations of the studio. The animals waited, their energies seeping into the dormant earth, while the sun gradually shifted south, gathering strength.

During this dark season I thought of Bear deep in some cave, dormant through her period of gestation. While a friend and I built my studio in the valley, Bear made her cubs in the mountain. Whenever I looked east to the mountains that winter I thought about the sleeping bears and the mystery of making. "God lies in the details" I repeated to myself, trying for perfect angles and exact measurements and right craftsmanship. God lies in the details of all growth and making. I was building my cave, my place to withdraw and hide, the sanctuary where I would birth my images and find God lying in the details.

O WATERS OF SALVATION
prove us, we beseech You

Shortly after Wolf was placed on the east altar in Maat I received this dream. It is dawn. Leaving the fire circle I see a large bundle at the entrance gate to my land. I open the gate to investigate. There is movement inside a burlap sack, and soft sounds. A litter of wolf cubs

emerges. They scamper into the corral and claim this place as their own. I spend the day in the corral under the cottonwoods watching them grow. As the day advances the seven pups grow to maturity. They are a pack of small, tough Mexican wolves. They see my dogs, but ignore them. The dogs cannot see the wolves or smell them. The wolves wander the area. The fence does not confine them, the spirit wolves simply move through it. They leave and return, leave and return and I adjust to their independence. They are not mine. I never touch them. Their otherness is an aura, an emanation which elicits wonder and respect. In turn they show an aloof respect for me. What I feel in them is not friendliness but a purposeful commitment. As they take possession of my land, I realize that they have been sent as guardians, keepers of my gate. The alpha female approaches and stares into my eyes. The intense contact awakens me. With such joy I cry out, "Ahhh, the wolves have come."

Come to stand at the threshold of the Porta Coeli and guard the entrance to the source. Darkness weighs into the moon and the sickle supports the weight of her fertile death, an ark filled with the seeds collected after the full moon flowering. The floating barque rocks and the seeds spill down into the blood clotted sea, down into the realm of Serpent, into the bed of regeneration.

O GUARDIAN OF THE LAND
hold us, we beseech Thee

My road ends in the river. In my lifetime I have been drawn to river cities and I have lived many years near some of the great rivers, the Mississippi and the Arkansas, and, in Europe, the Danube, the Arno and the

Severn. My road now ends in the Rio Grande. A wild preserve (still called *bosque*, the Spanish word for woods by a river) runs through the heart of this city of Albuquerque, a thick and wide green ribbon bordering the Rio Grande for thousands of acres.

I cannot imagine my life without this river and this bosque. My months are marked by the seasonal cycle of the cottonwood groves, the wild olive and the tamarisk, by the waxing and waning of the river's flow. Forever overpassed by sun and moon moving west into the desert, the Great River shimmers under their yellow gaze, even when it is churned and muddied by rainfall. When rain runs off the Jemez Mountains, the river colors rust red, staining my flesh and the dogs' coats for days. Fecund river blood washing my body and soul. Each day I enter the Great River and I am reborn in her waters. So it is not surprising that this holy place frequently enters my dreams. Protected in this magic place, I nurture a protectiveness toward it, and in my need to have it ever there I often dream of guarding the space and somehow maintaining its wild sacredness.

In this dream image I am in the bosque at night. I wander in the woods carefully carrying a large bundle which I cannot see or identify. It is not heavy and I am carrying it easily. Ahead is an opening among the cottonwoods where the ground is illuminated by the full moon. As I reach the light I look up and see a bird pass across the moon. I look down at the bundle and see that it is an immense nest and in the nest lies a gigantic egg. Glowing so huge and yellow it seems that I am holding the full moon in my arms. I continue to walk in the bosque thinking of the egg in my arms and the eggs in the bird's body, the eggs in the snake which I hear passing near my feet and the eggs in my body. All the eggs are part of the moon egg overhead. When I reach the river I wade in to waist depth and lay the nest into the current, rippling white in moonlight, and watch the egg float downstream.

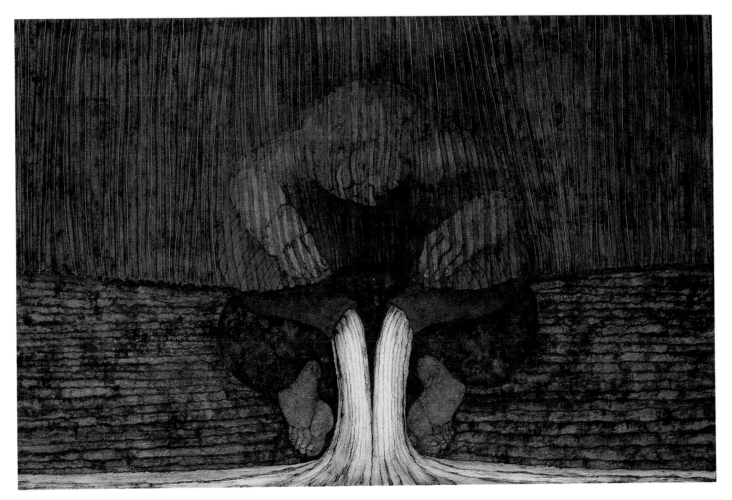

O ETERNAL WATER

sign us, we beseech Thee

The Great River flows in my life springing from God's throne and the fountainhead in Colorado mountains. Walking its banks I watch the egrets and plovers, the teal and mallards feeding and flying. I watch my dogs running, swimming, sometimes playing with beavers. I pass coyotes, already staring at me before I see them.

And while I am watching the animals and birds I am watching the river and listening. In the water I hear the aboriginal sounds which musicians and poets, shamans and seers have heard in the Great River from the beginning and repeated to their people. In the sound I hear their songs cast into the Great River a long long time ago. Music from the veiled source and these human melodies gather in the long bed waiting to be heard and retrieved by someone, somewhere downstream, in time. Adding to this eternal litany, I tell my own stories to the river, stories I have heard, dreams which people have entrusted to me, my own dreams, tales I have read. The words I write I take to the river and read to the water. Until I have given the words to the river they are not mine to give. Until they are thrown into the flow, washed and bedded in her body, I do not trust their purity. The water absorbs the sounds and the timeless commingling continues, running with purpose to union with all the waters circling this sweet earth. In the waters the sounds go round and round.

Sometimes I think of the animals hearing the songs in the water and perhaps understanding something good about us. I always carry with me one of my stone animals. Washed in the river, the animal returns the sound to its altar in the studio and the sounds in the stone sing like the stones in the riverbed.

O SOUL
OF THE WORLD
seal us, we beseech Thee

The music in the river returns to my studio and runs within the music which plays here all day, and into night. Music magnifies the aboriginal sound. It plows my soul, upturns my earth, reaches into ever deeper levels to dig out and irrigate the innermost memories. The great gorgeous sound enters the deepest well where live the fish with the largest eyes and lures images from the depths. Music verifies all I have ever understood about the searing beauty of the matrix.

In some of Mahler's music I hear the sound coming from the place where I know I live. Knowing that certain pieces are haunting me, I may wait for years for an image to arrive from this *ur* place where it has gestated, inspired by the music originating in the same matrix. Music is my psychopomp, guiding my images from the otherworld and attending their birth. The suite of paintings published as *The Mother's Songs* was inspired by some of the songs in *Das Lied von der Erde*, especially "The Farewell," the last, the longest, the most powerful evocation of the voice of the Divine Mother. For in Mahler's songs I first heard her singing to me. Through a span of eight years I passed countless hours absorbing her voice before the images in these paintings began to appear.

True to his name, Mahler is an iconographer; he makes the divine present in his song icons. Another of his icons that I worship before is the soprano's Resurrection Song in his 2nd Symphony. Early in the symphony a heart-rending two note instrumental melody is introduced, a cry from afar, a cry one must hasten toward. It vanishes in the forest but returns periodically through the long work. At last the simple piercing melody is articulated and the soprano cries, "O Glaube." O believe, my heart, O believe.

O CALL
OF THE WILD
return us, we beseech Thee

Was it a recurring day dream or night dream? I cannot remember. For a long time after my mother's sudden death I felt myself abandoned, the cord decisively cut this time, she flown, me rooted far away in a European monastery, lonely inside a high red brick wall. In the dream I am a severed branch stuck ungracefully in a pitcher of water. Over time the image recurs but evolves and the branch becomes a thick tree growing

on the bank of some river. My bark is tough and black, befitting my Benedictine garb. My tree torso is deeply rent with a gaping hole. The pain in this wound is unbearable. I cry constantly, crying for my mother. One night, or day, the picture comes for the last time and brings a healing magic. Something is alive within this painful wound.

I do not immediately recognize the bird for I have not seen a flicker for fifteen years. He flies directly into the hole in my body and feeds his young who are nesting within. Flicker has come from afar, from the west, across more than half a continent and an ocean. He has flown to me from the cottonwood groves along the banks of the Rio Grande where I last saw him. With his long thin beak he strikes. Come home, he says to me. In the rapid woodpecker drumming I hear the refrain repeated: Come home, Come home.

O GUARDIAN OF THE PLACE
see us, we beseech Thee

My four dogs race up the bank to the ditch and dance in expectation along the fence. Sitting under one of the great cottonwoods on my land, I watch them at some distance. Infrequently someone passes there to check the irrigation ditch for obstructions. But not now, not at twilight. And besides, the *acequia* is dry today, the ranchers are not irrigating their alfalfa fields. I expect to see another dog, or a cat, a skunk or raccoon, perhaps even a coyote alerting the dogs. But no animals pass by. Nevertheless the dogs gather at the gate, whining in anticipation, tails wagging a welcome. Who is there? The virgin moon hangs in the interstices of the cottonwood branches, scalloped by the large heart-shaped leaves. Then I notice that the crescent moon is directly over the gate. Do the dogs see this alignment? Are they welcoming the moon? Do they smell her? Then I, too, catch a glimpse of something at the gate, a movement, the air there has shifted. Leaves touched by a summer evening breeze moving up the valley? A nighthawk or an owl? Tall, well-watered ditch grass trembling? At that moment, by some instinct or leap of the imagination, I identify the presence. It is Artemis, the virgin hunter, and she has come for my hunting hounds.

I watch the moon traveling west for the rest of the evening. Before she crosses the Rio Grande I lose sight of her in the massed branches of hundreds of cottonwoods in full summer leaf. I watch her watching me. She hunts my soul and strikes my eye with that sharp crescent curve, a searing lunar cautery. I am branded. I am one of hers. I have the eyes of a solitary hunter. Then I understand her presence at my gate and gift of insight. Hunting is not about killing: hunting is about seeing.

Alone, we watch for tracks in our solitary journey. We trail our dream animals and stalk memories to the source. We stake out our innermost

landscape and we wait there, watching to see the creatures who may appear. We do not kill these wild creatures of our imagination. We coax them to follow us home. We entice them with whistles and songs and sweet humming and soft food pulped in our mouths. We stroke their feathers and fur and give them water from cupped hands. We feel for wounds and measure the fright in their eyes and heartbeats. Whatever Artemis allows us to see in this solitary landscape we may bring home. She gives her wild creatures to us. She tells them to do their silent and magic work, to burrow into our souls and hide in our hearts and make our eyes wild with vision. Whoever Artemis chooses to see is already a seer.

O HIDDEN GARDEN
enfold us, we beseech Thee

From April through October I sleep outside on a screened porch. I fall asleep with trees in my eyes and I awaken with trees in my eyes. There is usually a breeze blowing through the valley, moving up river from the south, stirring the high upper branches of the cottonwoods into my ears. I sleep outside to hear the sounds in the night.

And I hear the moon in her passing light and nightly transitions. I hear her light falling in the cottonwood leaves and I hear them spin on their long stems, answering. Regenerating herself, her excess splendor seeds the earth and each Tree of Life flowers. And then, like her, spills its seed. Falling down, I hear the light and the seeds falling down, and other sounds rising up from the waters hidden beneath this desert.

Great Turtle churns in sleep, shakes the roots of the earth, shakes my cot. When dawn breaks and I awake to the trees in my eyes, my ears are ringing with the night silence which sings in my solitude through the day.

O SEAT
OF WISDOM
enthrone us, we beseech Thee

Lady Wisdom threads the labyrinth of her womb and each of us begins our life journey to her center, our pilgrimage to the Holy Land. *Doth not Wisdom cry out? Doth not understanding put forth her voice?* throughout the moons of our life span?

There is a Mexican tale about a beautiful woman who came to live in a small village many generations ago. She taught the people how to live by the phases of the moon,

> to spin and plant under the virgin moon
> to weave and nourish under the full moon
> to finish and harvest with the dying moon
> to withdraw and pray at dark of moon.

The beautiful woman stayed with the people for many seasons. One night when the villagers were celebrating full moon, the woman, dancing ecstatically, took flight. Becoming a bird, she flew into the night sky, all the way to the moon. Then the people knew that it was Moon herself who had lived among them and taught them her wisdom.

O WELLSPRING
contain us, we beseech Thee

I have two guardian angels and I have called them Rose and Colette since childhood. My grandmother had a rose garden. In her rose garden one morning I clearly felt the presence of my guardian angel. Feeling for the first time the need to name her, I named her Rose, I think because the rose was the most beautiful flower in my summer days. My other angel is Colette, my baby sister. My mother bore four daughters. Colette, the last child, died in infancy. My sisters and I never even saw the baby but her life was very real because we shared our parents' loss. So Colette became a powerful presence in my imagination, my own special guardian angel, who still hovers over the birth of each new painting.

O ALMA MATER
name us, we beseech Thee

On the twelfth anniversary of our mother's *dies natalis* my two sisters were visiting from the midwest. At the entrance to this *alamosa*, this cottonwood grove, we planted a cottonwood tree to remember, again, the day our gracious mother was borne into heaven. So we named the tree Alma Mater. Especially tended and watered, already growing thick and high, Alma Mater guards my gate, she keeps my threshold, the place where I await my own *dies natalis*.

Through the years, from time to time, a woman walked through my daydreams and night dreams. She also appeared in many paintings, stayed briefly and then vanished into the subcutaneous layer of content. Distant, always moving left, never looking at me, she glided through the landscape, robed, carrying many roses. I never saw her feet and for some reason this puzzled me. Speaking to her, I began to call her Alma Mater, welcoming her, watching her strangely motionless passage. Then she appeared in a painting and stayed and I came to recognize her, a woman manifesting the journey into the crone moon, the journey into wisdom and regeneration. She does not need feet for she glides astride the body of the Serpent who is moving into its own phase of renewal, sloughing off a dead self, sliding out of an old mask.

O HOLY TRINITY
awaken us, we beseech Thee

When I was a child, reading the *Chicago Tribune* was an evening ritual. Sitting on the floor at my father's feet I paged through each section after he finished reading it and passed it down to me. I looked for photographs, photographs of anything which interested me, hoping especially for photographs of animals to draw from. I taught myself to draw by studying these newsprint images and drawing from them.

I had no desire to linger after school for any activity. I wanted to be at home drawing. In the late afternoons, before my father returned from work, my sisters and I sat on the floor around the high wood-box radio listening to the afternoon serials for children. Nearby, in the kitchen, our mother prepared the evening meal. As each serialized story unfolded in fifteen minute episodes, day after day, I drew the stories as I heard them and stapled them into "books." Leaning against the wooden box the sound vibrations came right through my back into the pencil. The Lone Ranger was the last and longest story, a heady half hour of horse hoofs beating on my back. My sisters and I hoped that our father would not arrive until 6:30 when The Lone Ranger ended. When he came home the radio had to be turned off.

Drawing became a daily habit. Drawing was necessary, something I not only wanted to do, but had to do, because it was through drawings that I communicated with my grandmother in Little Rock. From September through May, I drew pictures for my grandmother. From time to time I would select from the collection and my mother would send a package of drawings to her mother. My grandmother never thanked me for these drawings, but she acknowledged them with collections of her own. Fat envelopes would arrive stuffed with chronological clippings of two cartoon strips which ran daily in the *Arkansas Gazette*, "Jitters" and "The Katzenjammer Kids," cartoons unavailable in Chicago. I did not miss one episode of Jitters the monkey or those kids who spoke slang German, the "KKs" we called them. Methodically, day by day, my grand-mother cut the two four-frame strips from the newspaper and carefully assembled them to keep the running storyline intact. She was making "books," too. This faithful exchange of imagery between my grand-mother and myself kept us connected during the nine months we were separated each year. She never wrote "thank you," she never said "I like this one" or "My favorite drawing is . . ." But when I returned to my grandparents' home for the summer months there my drawings would be, taped to a wall in the dining room surrounding the only picture that hung in their home. This was a large dime-store print of a wolf in a snowy landscape, a great gray wolf howling at the moon. "Look, I give your drawings to Wolf and Moon," she seemed to be saying to me.

My grandmother died when I was twelve years old. But in the repeated summer journeys of return to her, the solitary figures of wolf, moon and grandmother became a unified, composite image which stirred and fer-tilized my imagination. Each was the other, a trinity of equals. Bound-aries, edges between these three silent presences slid away, revealing a trinitarian mystery of union which deeply marked my young soul. Credo, said my soul. Credo, say my drawings, still, today. I believe in this holy trinity of grandmother, wolf and moon and worship these an-cestral spirits deep within me.

O ROSA MYSTICA
enclose us, we beseech Thee

The mountains were still warm the evening when it happened. As the caves, mouths opened west, swallowed the setting sun, the full moon

rose over the mountains still bathed in the milky green silt of her underworld journey. The Blue Moon, second full moon of this summer month, floated up in a translucent aureole and tilted her face down to the mountains.

God speaks in these warmed cave temples. God says, Come into my enclosed garden. Come into my lap and sit in the center of your soul. Drink the living waters of memory and give birth to yourself. What you unearth will stun you. You will paint the walls of this cave in thanksgiving.

O YOU WHO GIVE THE DREAM
inspire us, we beseech Thee

In dreams we go down, as if pushed down into our depths by the hands of God. Pushed down and planted in our own inner land, the roots suck, the bulb swells. In her depths everything grows in silence, grows up, breaking the horizon into light. We rise up as flowers to float on the line between the above and the below, creatures of both places. She who gives the dream ripens the seeds which fly in the air and float in the water.

In my dreams I am often led down by Turtle, soul totem, who takes me deeper than I would dare and gives me the dream treasure to bring up to the horizon and into a painting. In my paintings the pattern appears again and again when the picture divides into equal halves and equal movements, above and below, and the horizon, like the dream, is the place of union.

O BEAUTY OF THE DEEP
sound us, we beseech Thee

The desert is green tonight under a winter full moon. The moon's light is green tonight like the light in dreams.

Like the green light in my friend Alice's dream as she looks out to sea. Alone, on a deserted shore, she watches a pregnant sea turtle struggle in from the sea. The turtle has pulled away from the maw of a deep whirlpool and, exhausted, she is near to death. In her body she carries the last seven eggs which any turtle will ever lay into the earth. She burrows, burying her seven leathery eggs. Alice drinks the tears from the mother turtle's eyes. Then she drinks the turtle's blood. It is a slow and agonizingly painful communion.

It is an infinitely sad dream my friend has written to me. I am so sad I cannot weep. Does the turtle lay her eggs in the shifting sands of our memories? When all the turtles are gone, will the eggs hatch only here? When an animal is extinct how long can it survive in human memory? And what may we know of *her* ancient memories? We can only hear what she tells us while she lives.

O PLACE OF EMERGENCE
bind us, we beseech Thee

The powerful archaic images of androgyny are difficult to look at. At least I am uneasy with them and I suspect other people are too. Any picture of half a woman side to side with half a man meant to represent a total human being at once fascinates, yet repels, depicting as it does something unnatural, indeed impossible, an aberration. What is it then that fascinates? Why do we stare at and investigate such images? Because the sign of androgyny shows us something which we feel is true but cannot comprehend or experience. What we gaze at is an artist's attempt at visualizing a mystery: the *coniunctio oppositorum*, the integration of duality.

The symbolic dual being in whom the opposing energies are united is a sign of Divine creative life. Each of us experiences this polarity in striving for our own completeness and equilibrium. It is the sign of the Mother-Father creative spirit within, and in each soul these energies are uniquely reconciled.

O ORIGIN
OF THE JOURNEY
guide us, we beseech Thee

In a boarding house room, near the Arkansas River, the two grand-mothers had attended the young woman since early morning. She was in a long, difficult labor with her firstborn, and her young husband at last asked them to fetch a doctor. The elderly doctor they found sent them all out of the room and they sat on the front porch of the boarding house, staring into the fog spreading from the river in the dark winter afternoon and listening to the rain and the cries of the young woman in the room off the porch. After some time the doctor came out and told the husband to go to the drugstore for some medication. When he returned he found the doctor curled into a corner of the room in a drunken stupor. Hearing shouts, the grandmothers entered the room and found the young man beating him. They pulled the old man out of the room and the husband locked the door.

So it was my father, alone with my mother, who at last received me from her body and put me into her arms. The next morning my father wrote his first letter to me. "Little girl I want just a word with you. This is being written when you are eighteen hours old. Your dear mother almost lost her life for you . . ."

O TREE
OF PARADISE
quicken us, we beseech Thee

I know a mother who returns to her ancestral home with her young daughter as often as possible each year. Sometimes they travel from Los Angeles by train, stopping here to visit on their way to Peoria. This mother is a storyteller and the child has always been enfolded in her mother's songs and stories. The mother's songs originate in her soil. Her soul flies and sings because her feet are grounded in her origins. Her feet are also grounded in the Riddle of Eternity.

Once upon a time I heard the story of a magical bird living in the branches of the Tree of Paradise and feeding upon its fruits. Thus the tree lives in the bird. The bird lays her eggs and within each egg spirals the life of the bird and the life of the tree and the life of the soil and the water that grew the tree. This is the Riddle of Eternity. Untold but contained in this story, completing the cycle, is the song of the bird. The bird which feeds upon the fruits of Paradise must sing.

So in their night flights, going home, the poets sing and the storytellers speak and the artists make pictures about the Riddle of Eternity. The riddle unwinds as a journey from the source back to the source. The mystery of the riddle is the eternal cycle, beginning and ending at the center in the entwined fingers.

Set upon this journey as an artist, from the laps of my own ancestors, I step along one painting at a time, unraveling the riddle, painting my way back to eternity, singing songs of thanksgiving and feeding from the Tree of Paradise.

O EYE
OF THE EARTH
search us, we beseech Thee

Birds do not cling for long. Earth is but half way for them, midway between the ancient waters of their genesis and the heavenly winds of a brief lifetime. They are messengers between here and there, binding humus and heaven, at home in both places. I need the sight of their flight. Birds penetrate the sky's depth, drawing invisible patterns, articulating the emptiness. They fly my eyes into winds and clouds and the crowns of the high cottonwoods. I scan the patterns they weave, chasing them into invisibility.

Predators, but also prey, such precise skill, flying and killing all day or night. Hard eye, beak, cry and claw. And in the morning I find earth strewn with the feathers and gut-pellets from last night's deaths. I gather them to feather the beaver sticks which I collect at the riverbank, narrow willow branches, sliced and stripped of the tender bark by the beavers who travel the banks at night. Sometimes earth needs planting with these feathered prayer sticks.

But finally earth does pull the birds down to herself. This afternoon a Downy woodpecker streaked into one of the large southern windows of my studio. I ran out. All morning, sitting at my work bench, I had watched him spiralling around an elm, stabbing grubs. Now the warm dead body seemed smaller in my hand than the live bird I had watched through the windows this morning. The head swung loosely from the broken neck and rolled over my fingers. Blood dripped then ran from the slightly open beak, collecting in my palm. After I had removed the wing and tail feathers, I buried the woodpecker at Crow's altar.

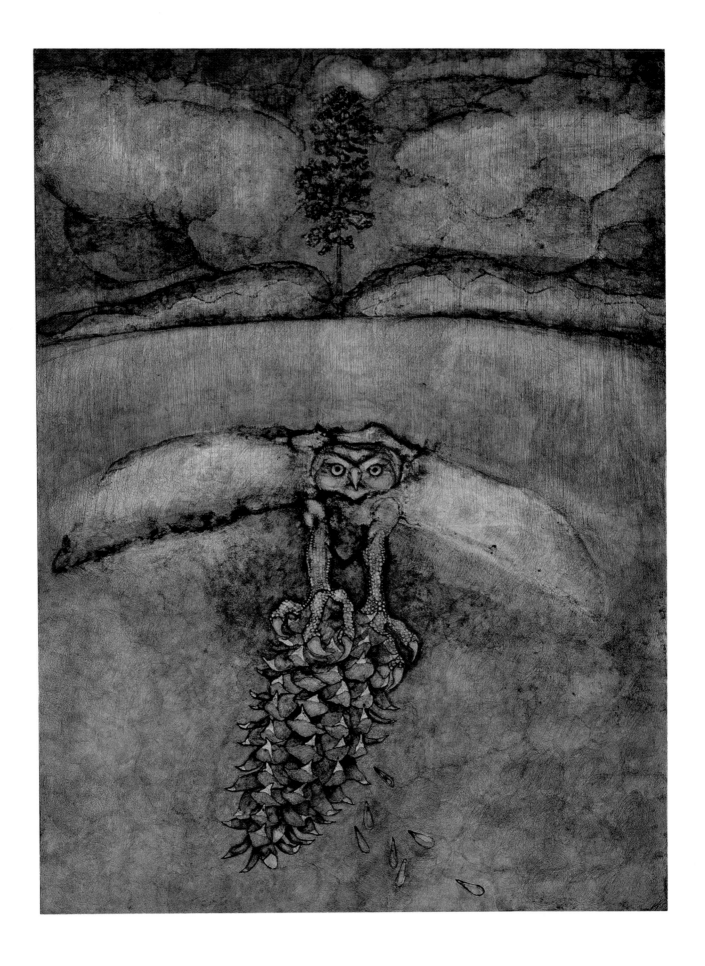

O SOUND IN THE STONES

call us, we beseech Thee

The loveliest moment of the drive home is the first sweeping view of the great sleeping turtle. As I drive down, dropping two thousand feet on the road from Santa Fe to the Albuquerque valley, she rests hugely on the southern horizon, her head tipped down to the Rio Grande, afloat in this vestigial ancient sea. Now this mountain is called Sandia but the indigenous Pueblo people once called it Turtle Mountain, when the land was theirs, and the names were theirs to give. They spoke of Turtle as the first creature to become; witness the seams in the shell where she came together, say some stories. Her steady balance in the primal ocean allowed the rest of nascent life to cling to her shell, to root in the mud on her back, to feed from the Tree of Life growing up from her carapace.

I drove up to Santa Fe with Elizabeth's portrait. In her father's family there is a tradition: a portrait is painted of each girl at her threshold time, when she steps across and is cloaked in her womanhood, when the Tree of Life flowers in her body and casts its first seed. This Wolf Clan child, who has named herself Turtle Woman, lives in the Sangre de Cristo Mountains near the place where the White Horse runs through the winter months.

O GUARDIAN OF THE DANCE
choose us, we beseech Thee

We danced the Dance of Death in my kitchen, between fire and water. That night, although I had heard nothing, I knew that someone was in my kitchen. Paralyzed with fear, I looked over at Erdamir for help but she was asleep. Why wasn't she reacting to this palpable presence in our home? I put down my book, ready to move, but I could not. I had to face whoever this was. I moved through the room toward the kitchen. She was standing at the threshold waiting for me to come and she took me into her arms. We began to dance, the Great Mother and I. My terror dissolved into her huge dark beauty, into her eyes fixed on me, into her divine laughter and the slow measured stepping in unison to music I could not hear. Her beauty was an ecstasy, a flowing current of bliss which I had never before experienced. Wild hair spilled over a mountain lion which lay across her shoulders, sometimes alive, sometimes a disembodied skin. Round and round we turned in the kitchen, staring into each other's eyes. I was aware that she had four arms and two hands came around my neck. She held me at some distance as if to protect our heavy bellies. Round and round we danced, with her hands increasing the pressure on my throat, diminishing my breath. She was going to kill me. Slay me, I said to her eyes. My soul surrendered saying, slay me. But my body did not. Then I had four arms and with two hands I began to strangle her. Round and round the slow dance continued, without struggle, a calm purpose driving us to complete this engagement. I obscurely understood that we were engaged in some ritual with which I was vaguely familiar. Breaking from her gaze I looked into the eyes of the mountain lion and slew the Great Mother. She vanished and I licked her sweet blood from my fingers.

I awoke from this dream trembling, weeping. The Night Mare had ridden into the center of my soul, into my very identity, and shaken my being.

Angry at her, bewildered, I tried several times to paint the visitation, but I could not grasp the contradictory levels of the experience. Some years later I finally painted the Dance of Death and in doing so I understood that the dream was the Dance of Life.

We had engaged in a solemn pomp, a sending forth. She sent out her power and strengthened me to contain it. She seemed to say, The power you possess is mine, you are my own divine self. As the painting neared completion, Mountain Lion appeared at the threshold of the kitchen cave, guardian of the mysterious exchange in the dance between the fire and the water.

O DESIRE OF THE ETERNAL HILLS
enchant us, we beseech Thee

She came in an I Am In New Mexico Again dream. Wandering across a mesa at twilight I saw, so improbably, a three month old German Short-hair puppy gazing at me from under a golden chamisa shrub. I squatted down, still at some distance, and began to speak to her. "Erdamir, Erda-mir, kommen Sie herein," I repeated softly. The incantation drew her into my arms.

Erdamir had told me her name and I knew that this Dream of the Earth was yet another summons to leave England and return to New Mexico. Shortly after I did so, several years later, Erdamir came into my home, a six week old puppy. She grew into a wild presence in my heart and the daily river run rhythm began in our lives. When she died five years later and was buried at the south face of the fire altar, she returned to my dreams where her eyes continue to burn my soul.

For she returned as a majestic *kachina*, her body huge and red, pierced with many coyote eyes, crowned with wild turkey feathers, her claws gigantic with earth energy. Now Erdageist, she lives in the land of the four red mountains, roaming with coyote, their wicked laughing eyes conjuring up earth spirits to roam in my paintings.

Today is the thirteenth moon of her passing over and I write this as a portion of the closure ritual. This morning I spaded her grave and planted a chamisa shrub. Aware that the dogs were not at my side, I looked up to the ditch bank and saw them lying there, watching me attentively. The poignancy of their quiet, focused presence caught at my heart, attending the ritual, as they were, with a gravity unusual for

them. Erdamir's daughter Akkama is her physical image but her wild and devoted heart beats in her son Brimos. A year later wherever I look there is still a hole where she was. Having Madra, her mate, and her two pups cannot assuage the ache of her loss. In the *O Fountain Mouth* painting, the first image which I attempted after her sudden and unforeseen death, she roiled out of the storm clouds surrounding the Great Mother's head, arched her body over the waterfall and poured her birthing blood and her death blood over her family.

Planting the chamisa over her body brings Dream of the Earth full circle but my chant to her continues. Erdamir, Erdamir, kommen Sie herein, kommen Sie herein. *O Thou Erdamir.*

O FOUNTAIN
MOUTH
purify us, we beseech Thee

Away on my long European sojourn, it was only in dreams that I could visit the Land of my Dreams. In them I often wandered this desert, these mountains, my Rio Grande valley. Like a wraith never laid to rest, the land returned to haunt my dreams and finally, after 21 years, to reclaim me. I had two magic carpets which served these dream journeys of return, two Navajo rugs which I had acquired when I lived in Albuquerque in the early 1960's. They were rolled up in my sister's attic in Milwaukee. In my dreams about New Mexico, the rugs unfurled and enfolded me in the flow of the Rio Grande and the four red mountains which their woven designs represented for me. These former household spirits floated through my dreamscapes determined to be honored and placated even in my absence. I missed the two rugs as I missed old friends and longed to see them.

Now the river rug hangs in my studio, above my workbench. Maat clothes herself in the waterfall and hides me in the grotto within the folds. The water spills down and fertilizes my creative space. She signs the boundaries with cornmeal. In the cave I pray, O Fountain Mouth, a cry I have whispered for such a long time, an icon given to me by Rainer Maria Rilke in one of his poems. Icon of the Fountainhead whence flow the divine waters from the Fons et Origo. Icon of the God of Beauty whom I worship, the dark God brooding over her waters, originating all life, blessing the growth rising from the matrix cast in her mold. *O Thou Fountainhead.*

L A U S   T I B I

CATALOGUE OF THE PAINTINGS

Page

15 HEART OF THE FIRE, 1989

17 HOUSE OF THE RISING SUN, 1987. Lucinda Thompson, Maine

19 GAZEHOUND HUNTS THE MOON, 1990

21 FLIGHT OF MAAT MOON, 1989. John Velasquez and
Neil McMinn, California

23 THE CHILDREN COME HOME, 1987. Margaret O'Brien Steinfels,
New York

25 CROW MOTHER OVER THE RIO GRANDE, 1988.
Penelope Farmer, England

26 SACRED HEARTS, 1990. Kathy Sage, New Mexico

29 WINTER SOLSTICE WOMAN, 1988

31 SEEDS OF REGENERATION, 1990

33 GUARDIAN OF THE EGG, 1987. Robert Lentz, New Mexico

35 THE WATERS OF LIFE AND DEATH, 1986. Susan R. Beehler,
New Mexico

37 THE SOUND OF THE RIO GRANDE, 1988. the artist

39 MY FLICKER CALLS ME HOME, 1990. The Rev. William and
Susan Flemr, Iowa

41 THE HUNTER COMES FOR HER HOUNDS, 1988

43 THE MOONS OF THE VERNAL EQUINOX, 1987.
Alice Zimmerman, Tennessee

45 HAGIA SOPHIA, 1987. Elaine J. Simard, New Mexico

47 SLEEPING WITH OUR MOTHER, 1988. Kathleen Kavanagh and
Colby Pfeil, Arizona

49 ALMA MATER, 1989. Mary Redman, California

50 THE GRANDMOTHER, 1987. Audrey Scotti, Connecticut

53 ROSA MYSTICA, 1988. Virginia Beane Rutter, California

55 SHE WHO GIVES THE DREAM, 1987. Joan L. Carlton, Kansas

57 JOURNEY WITH TORTUGA AND STORM PETRELS, 1986.
Alice Saunders, North Carolina

59   BIRTH RITE, 1987

61   SNAKE MOTHER ATTENDS THE CROWNING, 1989

63   NIGHTHAWK STORYTELLER, 1986. Mariclare Costello Arbus, California

65   PONDEROSA OWL TURQUOISE MOUNTAIN, 1988. The Rev. Betsy Alden, New Mexico

67   PORTRAIT OF ELIZABETH CLOW, 1989. Elizabeth Clow, New Mexico

69   GUARDIAN OF THE DANCE, 1989. Kathleen Kavanagh and Colby Pfeil, Arizona

71   COYOTE AND ERDAGEIST IN THE LAND OF THE FOUR RED MOUNTAINS, 1989

73   O FOUNTAIN MOUTH, 1989. Brian and Astrid Meldrum, England

The paintings are worked in scratchboard with drawing inks.
The originals measure approximately 12″ × 16″.

Offset lithography prints of some of the paintings in this book are available from: Casa Alamosa, 2712 Campbell Road NW, Albuquerque, New Mexico 87104.